My Urban Oasis

My Urban Oasis

#walking #nature #trees #breathing
#sensations #inspiration #free
#mindfulness #body #heart #mind
#happier

Anne Marceau Jacquet

My Urban Oasis
Copyright © Anne Marceau Jacquet 2019
All rights reserved.

Edited by Camille Jacquet and Doreen Wang
Artwork by Anne Marceau Jacquet
Book Design by Anne Marceau Jacquet

For information, please contact: www.amjconsulting.net

ISBN: 9781078452717

To Julien

My heartfelt gratitude to:

Camille and Julien,
Brenda, Eleni, Raleigh, Sara, Teresa,
Catherine,
Karine,
Zhu Ping,

Thank you for sparking the idea for this book, for supporting, encouraging, sustaining, correcting, editing, re-editing, reassuring and much more....

Without you, this book would not exist, and I would not be the same.

Opening Invitation

My Urban Oasis
Is an invitation to a promenade,
A search for peace and well-being,
An exploration of forgotten sensations,
The discovery of unexpected beauty in nature.

It is a story that tells how to release tension
To lift the weight of life,
Welcoming all things
Without judgment.

For an instant, a moment,
To choose,
To be present at this time and place,
Now and here,
Nowhere else,
Nothing less, nothing more.

Part I: The Journey

A New Ritual

E very morning, for the last three years, I walk. I do not run or jog; I don't even walk fast. No hiking stick, no Fit Bit, no earphones, just my body and my mind. I walk slowly enough to feel my body, to watch whatever is around me, and to listen to the silence as well as the sounds. I walk with little purpose other than walking. I do not have any expectations for results—no sweat or muscle building. I just be with myself and feel that I am here—paying attention to my own body, being aware of my own breath, feeling the ground— the bouncy soles of my sneakers, the soft sensation of my socks, even the gentle stretch under the arches my feet.

I reconnect with my sensations as well as with the surroundings, with the nature all around, with the light of the sky, or the shadows of the clouds, whatever is here.

I usually begin by putting attention on my physical sensations: the air that I breathe, the rhythm of my inhalations, and the loosening of my body when I exhale. I can feel my muscles relaxing and softening.

Then, I direct my attention to each step and how I feel in each little part of my body: my arms hanging freely at my sides and my body straight-aligned and symmetrical. Ah, just the right sensation—that the weight of gravity is content at its minimum and there's a sense of lightness without restraint. Now, I am reconnected with my body.

Surprisingly, by walking every day in the same park, I discover an unsuspecting world. Actually, I knew that this world existed, but I had totally underestimated its full dimensions. Each slow walk turns out to be a full-fledged exploration, even though this trip just takes place within steps of my door. It has been a journey inside myself as well as with the outside world.

What I had not foreseen was the satisfaction that I would feel watching very small and mundane details within the park. As I breathe deeply, I watch the life around me with great care. All my senses are alert! I can spot a butterfly, or even two who fly like a loving couple, one after the other. I notice one bird singing, other birds in another direction responding to each other, and squirrels in the trees making funny squeals. It took me several weeks before I could identify them. Every day in the same park, I would come across a special discovery that would surprise and delight me.

I had never thought that I would treasure doing the same thing in the same place every day! I pay attention to every element present at the moment: the fresh air on my skin, the breeze and wind, or the warmth of the sun touching my shoulders. I try not to miss anything—especially the fragrance of the Osmanthus trees. It is often impossible to identify which specific branch is the source of this mysterious scent.

Because the contemplative walk is slow, it allows the focus to rest on the flow of air, the physical sensations now and here, and the sensory perceptions of the surroundings. Then the mind slows down, unwinds, finds peace, and revitalizes.

Why

I can't really say that I freely chose to follow a slow routine. This practice was the result of several years of back pain and general body aches. Despite various attempts to find a physical activity that could help relieve the pain and keep me in shape, my condition deteriorated. I had to stop going to the gym; I could not go hiking anymore. Swimming was not doing me any good either. I tried yoga, Pilates, stretching, but somehow I would injure my body more with whatever I was doing! No activities seemed suitable to my condition. Working and going on with my daily life were also painful. I was frustrated and desperate. What could I do? Not moving was not an option. Sitting was even more painful and terribly depressing!

How could I reconcile two forces in my life that, for many people, may not seem to be conflicting? One side was leading the active life I wanted, with work, children, family, friends, a few hobbies and passions—in my opinion, nothing extraordinary! The other side was finding the ability to maintain a reasonable level of energy and a physical and mental balance to be active this way. But as I slowly slipped into a state of chronic pain and severe fatigue, the only way I could describe how I felt was a constant state of contradiction. Any and every activity was getting more challenging by the day, and balance was becoming a goal always out of reach.

Desperate to retrieve a normal life and normal "me" back, I tried testing out a few different activities. I started to practice deep breathing and mindfulness exercises. I had read books about mindfulness and had participated in few sessions with an instructor but was still unsure that it could be an accessible activity for me, something that would fit my way of actively engaging with life and my yearning for movement and rhythm.

Other times, I practiced very mild stretching—something closer to relaxation rather than fitness. In addition, I began to have this feeling that walking slowly might help with my overall physical distress.

I started to walk in a way that focused on bodily perceptions at every step. Looking for ways to reduce pain, I placed one foot after another on the ground and carefully observed what each of my senses could perceive. Gradually, I developed the ability to more precisely identify and feel the various muscles, joints, and tendons on my legs and back. I wanted to give time and space to my body to express whatever sensations may appear, and meanwhile, give my mind the time and space to free itself from thinking.

Slowness was a method with which to experiment deep breathing while walking. With great delight, I found that deep breathing and slow-paced walks were well-suited for each other; and that the park near my home held the potential to unfold an unexpected dimension to my routine.

It so happened that I also began to find an effective medical treatment for my ailments around the same time I started my daily walks. However, I believe that the healing would not have been possible if one had happened without the other. The medical support made walking possible, and the walking made my body more receptive to medical treatment.

"My" Park

I was born in France but have lived in Taiwan for many years. Taipei, the capital city where I live, is far from the size of some of Asia's huge metropolises; however, in all respects, the pace of life is not slow. The city has a dense urban population of three million people, a workforce scrambling to stay competitive in a rapidly developing region, and constant, heavy traffic—with tons of scooters running around in a hysterical dance 24 hours, seven days a week. Nevertheless, Taipei holds a great treasure—its mountain ranges. It is bordered on three sides by low-range mountains covered with tropical vegetation. The north side of the city is marked by the Yang Ming Mountain Range, the highest mountain range in all of northern Taiwan and is now a designated protected area, Yang Ming National Park. It is reachable by public buses and is the perfect place to hike or just enjoy nature and some peace. The city's realm spreads midway up the mountains, making it possible for people to live near or on Yang Ming and still be reasonably close to the city center.

What I consider to be "my" park is actually a public city park located on a slope halfway up the top of one of the Yang Ming mountains. Although not very steep, it provides a hilly landscape and a variety of scenic views. It is also an experimental horticultural park that is designed to breed and exhibit various species of flowers, trees, and plants. The park is plotted in sections, each dedicated to one main species, and separated—not with a fence or a physical wall—but with forest paths that serpent in between. The floor map of the park is a funny mix of square grids and free designs, with paths that meander, zigzag, and wind freely throughout. It does not cover a large area but is very dense and offers a wide variety of flora. The many alleys and lanes that canvas the park grounds give the walker many intriguing options and make it a favorite destination for photographers and nature lovers of all ages.

The entrance is very modest. It can easily go unnoticed from the busy road that connects the mountains to the city. But once you step foot inside, you are welcomed by an impressive camphor tree that spreads its branches over your head, offering generous shade during the hot months and makeshift shelter from drizzles during the rainy season. Over time, this camphor tree becomes an important friend to me.

The camphor tree leads to the park's main walkway, lined with trees on both sides and foliage that meets high above one's head, creating a green tunnel that stretches in a straight line toward the opposite end of the park. A majestic view! Newlywed couples who come here for their wedding photography have a perfect setting with which to mimic their entrance into a cathedral.

The park is home to many species of trees and shrubs; they are green all year round except the cherry trees which remain bare until they revive with spectacular bloom in the spring. The park's camellia collection is also impressive—incredible in their variety of shapes, sizes, layers, textures, and of course, colors. The blooming cycle of the most eye-catching flowers is very well planned. After the camellias come the cherry blossoms, followed by the azalea flowers which stay on display for the better part of summer. This, of course, is in addition to smaller seasonal flowers which are planted on the sides of the walkways and which renew each season.

But this park is not a museum. It is not a still or excessively groomed piece of art. It has a friendly and casual feel, an unassuming and unpretentious atmosphere that may partly be due to the presence of modest and rather unsightly buildings: greenhouses, educational centers, exhibition halls, and workshop spaces where gardeners design, prepare, and maintain the park experiments. Experiment is a good word to keep in mind, because most of all, it is a place that breathes with its own, dynamic life.

Angles & Perspectives

I have walked each and every path of the park. To make my walk slower and longer, I follow several itineraries that meander in zigzags, giving me the time and opportunity to familiarize myself with every corner. With great care, I have identified several different spots where I find the view of the surrounding mountains to be the most breathtaking and inspiring. Sometimes, however, I still discover new places and perspectives, where the mountains appear to me with a new face. In those moments, I always find myself surprised by such delightful discoveries and feel as if I were walking in the footprints of a magical explorer, capable of seeing the new and exceptional in everyday simplicity.

Angles are very important, I've come to learn. From one angle to another, the same scene will produce a different picture and may, consequently, trigger different perceptions. This is partly why photography is classified as a visual art. The taking of each and every photo is unique and may bring about a different feeling. The framing of a photo presents a scene, a specific view, which at times, may look dramatically different from "reality." The way my eyes contemplate scenery feels similar to a camera lens. The frame of my vision adjusts and changes according to the angles and perspectives of my location, and, almost as if by magic, the same landscape may produce an unexpected surprise.

Sometimes, while walking on one of the main paths, I will turn my head and be startled by the discovery of a new view. One morning, I was practicing stretching exercises at one of my usual spots. I love this remote corner, away from the flow of the other passersby and wedding photographers. I appreciate its shade under beautiful trees and the view I have from this elevated point. That morning, as I stretched my upper body, bending arms and shoulders toward the ground, I twisted my neck in the opposite direction up toward the sky. In this posture, I could see the upper branches of the tree with the blue of the sky seeping through. Wahoo! Such a beautiful and unexpected image! An ephemeral snapshot that delighted me as it came and went in a blink.

Movements

I have some hesitations saying that I walk in mindfulness. However, if mindfulness implies attention to breathing, consciousness of my sensations, awareness of my present emotions, concentration on the moment...then mindfulness is a part of my morning walk. I was inspired by the beautiful book, Méditer au Jour le Jour by Christophe Andre; it was a life-changing reading for me. I have mainly practiced mindfulness by myself—using guided audio exercises and practicing occasionally with an instructor—and I am far from an expert.

Most mindfulness, meditation, and contemplative practices I have been exposed to are often done while seated. While I was very much attracted to the potential benefits of mindfulness practices, staying still was and has always been difficult for me. Rather, being on the move is what has always brought me a sense of excitement. Therefore, intuitively and spontaneously, my routine developed in a way that combined walking, consciousness of my breathing, inward and outward contemplation, and mild stretching exercises.

At some point during the walk, I typically stop by an elevated spot with a special view. It seems essential to me to look out at the mountains and check how they are each day. By definition, mountains do not move; they are still and are supposed to look the same for centuries and millennia. However, the conditions of weather, light, and visibility also change, and hence, produce a unique image of the mountains every day. To me, the mountains are like friends. I look at them and talk to them: "How are you today? Oh dear! You're in the clouds!" I know them enough to feel deeply connected to them, and even if they look different from one day to another, I feel reassured by their soothing presence.

Once I have chosen a good spot, I exercise; I follow a routine of favorite movements in a very slow and focused way. I feel the flow of energy in my body and in the surrounding space. It resembles the breeze in the air, blowing with its own path, unknown and indeterminable to us. Energy is the flow of life, invisible but perceptible.

As I do my exercises, I observe the sensations I feel and my connection with the nature all around. I practice stretching and breathing, while staying completely focused. I bend and touch the ground to feel the temperature and the roughness of the ground; if I open my eyes, I can sometimes spot small insects going on their way. And I smile!

Sometimes I stand still, straight but not stiff, in a balanced posture with which I can hold myself upright without any effort. Breathing in a natural rhythm, I feel the energy flow like a vertical current that spirals from the ground upwards. I can close my eyes or let them wander freely to catch a glimpse of colorful flowers or the delicate movement of a butterfly in the distance. I notice the birds chirping, the breeze rustling in the foliage, the song of the cicadas, or a sudden silence.

When I conclude my session, I have the sense of awaking from another world. It is a strange and fascinating sensation. I wake up feeling totally fresh and anew. Mindfulness or not, my practice is a contemplative attitude toward my inner self and the universe around me. When I feel so intimately connected to the world, I can relate to the Taoist theory of the universe, which is governed by currents of energy that are called Qi. This concept finally becomes lucid and more approachable.

Traceless

M y body is usually still sleepy or rusty when I step out my door. I need to wake her up gently. Moreover, because of my sore muscles and tight joints, it feels as if my footprints on the ground would also trigger pain imprints on my body.

I walk slowly and lightly to produce the least amount of pressure possible, hoping that if bodily movements are lightened, then perhaps physical discomfort could be alleviated and harsh impacts on the body could be prevented as well. So, I glide or float, discretely and humbly, as if I were walking on a velvet carpet. I move carefully and contemplatively to not disturb the fragile equilibrium of my own self, as well as the nature all around.

These simple moments make me question the futility of human beings' desire to leave traces of their passage in the world and in people's lives. When I walk, I am an observer instead of a player, willing to contemplate instead of doing. For one hour, one hour only, I am totally detached from pursuing any aim other than paying attention to the present moment. Time has stopped, or maybe not time, but my focus on the social world and its insisting requests. I walk for the sake of walking. Just being a passerby, nothing more, nothing less.

The Connection through

Trees

T he big camphor tree at the park entrance welcomes
me, still and silent. It has opened its arms to me from
the very first day of my walks. I admire the shape of
its large trunk and big branches that have grown toward the sky.
I observe the strength of life that expresses itself through those
branches—a powerful desire to grow toward the sky. Trees are
a very physical expression of life; and each species expresses
this in its own way through the peculiar shapes of its trunk and
branches.

I have gradually developed a fascination for trees. My
special connection with trees began with this majestic camphor
and since then, I've become a tree aficionado. They are
captivating and so friendly. They come in unusual and
extraordinary shapes, impressive sizes, and convey strength
and confidence. They are so diverse; even among the same
species, each tree grows in its individual way, showing its own
personality. Maybe because they stand upright and tall in a
vertical posture, some feel almost human. They have bark like
we have skin, branches like arms, and roots like feet.
Sometimes, it seems that there is a face hidden in the shape of
the trunk or between their branches. Their sap runs through

conducting tissues, bringing nutriments and water, just like the blood circulating in our vascular system and veins. I speak to them, touch them, and smell the fragrance of their perfume. The wingspan of their foliage is also very welcoming. It protects us from the rain as well as the glare from the sun.

I had been walking in my park for over three years when my curiosity about trees guided me to undertake further learning with the help of two books: The Hidden Life of Trees by Peter Wohllenben and Shinrin Yoku: The Art and Science of Forest Bathing by Dr. Qing Li. The Japanese concept of Shirin-yoku feels very close to my style of contemplative walking in "my" park.

The practice of Shinrin-yoku first appeared in Japan in the 1980s; participants not only walk in the forest but also deliberately engage with the natural environment. While walking, they practice deep breathing and concentrate on the natural elements that surround them and attract their interest. They actively interact using their five senses. Some scientific studies claim that Shinrin-yoku can help support health and wellness. There is now research on exposure to Phytoncides, volatile compounds released by plants that help trees communicate among themselves. Phytoncides exposure is also purported to have beneficial health benefits for humans, such as reducing stress hormones.

Blue Mountains

T he slopes of the Yang Ming Mountains are covered by a thick subtropical forest. Abundant vegetation grows in every corner. It is a lush paradise where green is the dominant color. All shades of green are represented all year long. There is, however, also blue in the green of the mountains. In traditional Chinese painting, the mountain ranges are depicted in multiple hues of misty blue. When I walk in the park, I travel in a world that feels like those painted scenes, moving as if I were in a dream. The fog that envelops the mountain makes it mysterious and unreal. I had long believed that Chinese landscape paintings represented scenes in the artists' dreams, but now, when I contemplate the mountains in the distance, I tell myself: "You see, ancient painters were depicting reality. Chinese mountains are blue! Now you see it! It is real!" I am fascinated by the way traditional Chinese painters have mastered an art of depicting mountains through a dreamlike lens, while actually offering a very close representation of reality; it is not a fantasy of their imaginations. Now I watch these mountains with tenderness, allowing my thoughts to wander across the strait of the real and unreal world, between dream-like portrayals of reality and the striking resemblance of reality to our dreams.

When I was 18 years old, one of the deep motivations that guided my choice to study Chinese was the intuition that Chinese philosophy would lead me to uncover a dramatically different way to view and perceive the world. While I was never tempted to become a scholar nor spiritual devotee of Chinese philosophy, a Taoist interpretation of our world has long since resonated with my sensibilities. As I walk watching the mountains and the river of clouds above, as I feel the wind or the breeze on my skin, as I look at the trees' branches being pushed in one direction and bouncing back as soon as the winds change direction, I can't help but imagine that energy currents—visible or invisible—are everywhere around me.

Concentrating on my breathing has also helped me feel the currents of energy that go through my body. Contemplating nature is another way to hone my perception of the vital energy of the world.

Contemplation

T here is always something going on in my mind. Thoughts are coming and going, reminiscing about the past while sometimes already anxious for the future. It is so easy to be carried away and to fail to be present...in the present. Contemplation is a way to feel intensely present, to ground in reality, to feel my presence inside and out.

When I watch contemplatively, I connect with the real objects and creatures that populate my immediate surroundings. I am in the real world and stop wandering in my mind. My eyes sweep a full 180 degrees across the visual landscape in front of me, spotting images and other visual cues that catch and sustain my attention: things that move or colors that provoke an impression or emotion. I might also capture and identify the sounds that flow to my ears, or acknowledge the sensation of the air, or the temperature of the breeze on my skin.

I try to stay in this state as long as it can last, until that inevitable moment where a new flow of thoughts brings this to an end. The human mind is made up of a continuous flow of thoughts that come and go often without apparent logic. This instinctive activity is automatic, often unconscious. It can be annoying as it distracts me and carries me away from my contemplation. I wish I could rest my mind on demand!

However, contemplation does not have to be defeated by such fleeting thoughts. After a moment of distraction, the mind can gently bounce back. Upon realization that my mind has strayed, I contemplate the disruptive thought and say to myself: "Hum…this is what crossed my mind. Ah ah! This is the thought that does not want to take a rest even for a little while!! Hum…let it be, and for now, let's go back to my peaceful contemplation…." Without any judgment I observe those thoughts coming and going, slightly disruptive but nevertheless, unable to prevent me from returning to my contemplative promenade.

City & Clouds

My ritual movements began even earlier than the exploration of "my" park in Taipei. One summer, while visiting family in Paris, I started to practice soft and slow workouts, made up of gentle stretching movements as well as deep breathing exercises. I exercised in the simplest way, in front of my wide open window. The landscape from my window had little to no connection with nature. The view was bright and pleasant, but I had difficulties spotting any green landscape. The trees, which lined the street at the foot of my building, were still young, with meager foliage. At least being on a higher floor gave me the advantage of having a view that embraced the rooftops of the traditional Parisian low-rise buildings and the sky above. I like Parisian roofs. They are one of the city's signature touches, which make Paris, "Paris." Observing them made me feel so much in touch with the unique atmosphere of this city.

Even if the roofs are an iconic part of the city's identity, when practicing my routine exercise, I found myself yearning for a connection with nature. Occasionally I would glance in the distance at the flight of a pigeon or two. The sky, and specifically the clouds, attracted my attention. They seemed to have a life of their own, as they made their way across the horizon, metamorphosing themselves in the process. They exemplified the concept of life as impermanent, where everything is ephemeral. This sky that lay in front of my eyes

43

at this precise moment was unique; in a minute, even in a second, it would not be exactly the same, and it would never come back exactly as it had been. Contemplating the clouds in their journey encouraged me to cherish the moment at hand, paying attention solely and solemnly to the present.

Since then, sky and clouds have been my faithful companions. They are everywhere. No matter where I am, as long as I can raise my eyes, I can contemplate them and instantly feel connected to the present moment. Wherever I am, in the city or in more natural surroundings, I know that a view of the sky will help me feel the breath of life.

During my sessions of deep breathing and stretching exercises, the open window let the wind, the sky, and the appeal of the outdoors come closer to me. I realized that what I was craving was walking; and I slowly began to change my routine to a mindful walk in the forest park located on the outskirts of my Paris neighborhood. I just walked slowly while breathing, and whenever I felt like the urge, I would stretch my tense muscles. This emerging ritual brought a new dimension to my life, adding value and quality to my daily routine. When I returned to Taipei, I found "my" park down the street from my home and since then, have adopted it as the beloved home for my practice.

Welcoming

I walk essentially because I like it. It is a pleasure of mine. I do not have expectations. I take whatever comes to me—birds songs as much as traffic noises in the background. My eyes freely wander here and there. Any living creature can captivate my attention—even so-called "creepy" insects or "slimy" worms. I am often amazed by spiders, fascinated by their cotton-like webs that envelop small bushes, not to mention the ants which crawl around my feet when I exercise.

I try to welcome the beautiful and the ugly—the burning sun, the sweat, and the chilly rain. It does not mean that I like the ugliness, the traffic noises, or the fumes but I like the walk no matter what I meet on my way. Welcoming chance or the random, noticing everything—the lovely and the undesirable—I learn to accept the fact that things are not perfect. Perfection and beauty—those are interpretations, but not reality.

Meanwhile, I am conscious of the gift I do have—that such a park exists almost at the foot of my door in Taipei. In the early stages of my practice, I often wondered, if in different circumstances, would I be able to welcome all and everything? How much would I appreciate my walk if it were not in my park? However, when I traveled and stayed in other cities, I found that I naturally began to adjust my walk for other urban environments. Everywhere I go, I try to make time to discover a new local place where I can practice my walk. Often, I am able to find a suitable green space, whether a city park or a river bank; and I welcome this opportunity for new discoveries

.

Novelty Lies in the Familiar

I am amazed to realize how careful attention and contemplation can bring novelty and surprise to some very familiar surroundings or daily routines. One day, as I returned to Taipei after a weeks-long trip, I had such a simple and genuine pleasure observing the way the wild grass and weeds had grown under the camellia trees. There are several dense plots where tall, mature camellia trees are planted. Usually, the dirt under and around the trees is covered with dry leaves from the previous season. However, the strong and vivid summer sunlight that year was powerful enough to stimulate the growth of grass, even in remote, dark areas. This realization was delightful. It conjured to mind the picture of a clearing in the middle of a forest, so natural, uncontrolled, and wild.

In one of the alleys that I had not passed by for a long time, I noticed with amazement that the "sleeping" tree lying on the ground had now grown to such an extent that I needed to walk around it. It took up most of the alley, leaving only a tiny space for a person to walk through. One year ago, a ferocious typhoon hit Taipei and many large and old trees were knocked down. My park was not spared, and a significant number of trees were laid down to the ground. Sadly, in downtown Taipei, there was no other option than to cut many of the fallen trees, leaving huge empty spaces on the sides of the roads. But here, in the park, the administrators have opted for an alternative solution. They have covered the base of the tree with additional earth and soil to preserve the roots. When it was possible, they propped up the tree trunks with wooden stilts, leaving the tree in a diagonal posture. In some other cases, they let the trees lie on their sides, forming an unusual installation of a slanted forest. Whether diagonal or horizontal, I learned that trees continue to find ways to live and even noticeably, to grow.

The Cicada' Symphony

I n the summer, the cicadas' songs are like an electrifying music piece. I can't say for sure if the colorful songs I hear all day long around my home, and with even greater volume during my walk, comes from cicadas or crickets. They keep their secret as I don't have the chance to see them while they produce their chant. They hide in the trees, in the deep of the bushes. Also, because their sound is diffused, it is almost impossible to figure out exactly where their song comes from. In one moment, I am certain that their melody is strolling to me from my right ear, and at the next moment, I'm sure I'm hearing it from behind me.

But as I walked during the warm summer days, my ears improved in their attention span and acuity. I came to the realization that there are many variations in the orchestra.

In the morning, there is often a duet of individuals. Two cicadas have a dialogue, answering in response to one another. The tempo changes as well as the source of the song. It bounces from right to left, from one insect to the other. Other times, the cacophony comes as the result of several duos, singing together or, may I say, on top of each other, as a conductor is most likely not appointed. The rhythm of their song reminds me of the cute, rhythmic sound of an old steam engine—"chuchuchu"—with its various speed accelerations. However, in the afternoon, their cacophony is explosive. It seems that there are thousands of them, everywhere in the trees, up and down, here and there. They are a symphonic orchestra furiously playing under the lead of a crazy conductor. Their sound is strident and screeching and leaves no moment or space for breathing. Their concerto gives a dynamic rhythm to my walk. Surrounded by their wild and strong presence, I feel immersed in the forest.

Just Feeling Good

I started to walk with no other purpose than finding a physical activity that did not trigger aching. But I persisted because it feels good. Yes! Not only do I continue to walk but I also look forward to it every day.

As I walk slowly, I witness my emotions and let them be as they are at that time and place. Contemplating my body as well as my mind, without any judgment, I feel alive. It is magical!

I am sometimes puzzled by the societal pressure that pushes people to be results-oriented. If it is societally understood and expected that things be done for a reason, is it also an absolute necessity to have a well-defined purpose for every action?

My contemplative walk is the fruit of an opposite logic. I give voice to spontaneity and freedom. I feel free from physical tension and free from social pressure. During that hour on my own, I can live a moment of disinterest from any materialistic intention. I leave life to chance, take what comes to me, and immerse myself in my sensory perceptions.

It is funny to see how unpremeditated actions may have positive side effects. Besides a greater sense of health and wellness, these moments dedicated to myself have improved my focus and sharpened my sense of sight and hearing. I have developed greater sensitivity on my skin, stronger kinesthetic perceptions, and a keener sense of smell. My skin is aware of temperature and climate changes, such as a crispness or dullness in the air or a gentleness or vitality in the wind. I have reawakened my sense of smell; I hardly miss the fragrance of a flower blooming, even if it is hidden discreetly in some thick bushes. All my senses are now on the lookout for new and unexpected discoveries within my body as well as in the outside world.

Friendly Encounters

E very day, regardless of the time of the day, I make several encounters with small animals, spiders, or butterflies, as if meeting friends that randomly cross my path. To my surprise, I can often also spot very tiny insects crawling on a branch, an ant walking on the ground, or more rarely, croaking toads calling out to each other. Often, a rustle in the bushes startle me; and then, I laugh at myself when I realize that it was only an innocuous lizard, a noisy toad, or a bird standing still, on the watch for its prey. I feel privileged, as if I were alone on the face of this earth. In my park, animals are not only encounters; rather, they have become my companions. They don't disturb my walk; and I don't intrude on their life either. I just enjoy passing by them. I smile at them and watch them go their own way.

They can be a distraction but at the same time, in order to notice them, I need my full attention and concentration. Otherwise, they are often so discreet that were it not for my full concentration, I would not see or hear them. Then, the world would not be as full of life. My walks would not be as surprising and exciting.

On one particular walk, I found that it was a day for couples and lovers. A recent storm may have generated some electric excitement and energy. I stared with amusement at the ballet of dragonflies around the lily pond—always two by two, one chasing the other, in a frenetic dance. Dragonflies are particularly challenging for human eyes, because they move like helicopters, changing directions in a blink. They hook my attention with their speed and their unusual color—a deep, dark, beautiful red. On that particular day, two dragonfly couples of another species flirted around the pond. I was impressed by their tiger-like yellow and black stripes and fascinated by their four transparent wings that vibrated like helicopter blades.

All year long, the pond is covered with lily pads. They spread to form a unified green cover across the pond, on which occasional lily flowers sprinkle dashes of yellow or purple. Below this green blanket, there are aquatic plants that float while also striving to sink their roots into deeper and more secretive layers of the pond. Most of the time, the water surface is very calm and still. Only minuscule tadpoles bring gentle activity to the water. Only very rarely can I catch a glimpse of one of the Koi carps that come to the surface in search of some insects to gobble. I know that three of them live hidden under the lilies. I cannot explain why, but during one particular week, I found the three of them searching across the surface of the water and sometimes breaking through the lily pads to pop up their heads. Their behavior triggered my curiosity and fascination. Why were they behaving in such an unusual manner? Was it the season, the extreme heat, a natural phenomenon, or an unusual attitude? Will I ever know?

Neither Success nor Failure

I n the flow of the day, making space in my mind for a walk is not always automatic. It can be challenging to free my mind from a certain task at hand, whether it is a work assignment, a family discussion, or a formal or informal meeting. I often find myself caught in what happened before and what is to be done next—entangled between past and future.

Some days, it seems like I "suffer" from an attention deficit—like a naughty child who does not conform to social expectations and act according to social norms. As much as my lack of attention is frustrating, I try to accept it with indulgence too. Wandering thoughts might be annoying, but do they really matter? If I watch them without judgment, I can acknowledge them and let them come and go. Do they prevent me from walking and breathing? Staring at colors and movement from wind? Not necessarily.

Between distractions, I can still enjoy the walk, the breeze, the smell of leaves, and the movements of the branches. There is no successful or unsuccessful walk; there are only walks.

Loving Couples

I often pass by newlywed couples taking their wedding snapshots. Their lovely postures and poses make me smile and fill me with a light mood.

As a matter of fact, the park has many different visitors: strollers, hikers, wanderers, photographers, even groups on botanical tours. But it is understandable that this beautiful little park has also been chosen by professional photographers as the ideal stage for wedding photography.

Some days, my walk takes the zigzag feel of a cross country race with tours and detours to avoid bumping into half a dozen or so loving couples posing like princesses and knights. I have to take side paths to branch off. Of course, their presence limits my freedom as I need to adjust myself to avoid to crossing into their photo shoots. Nevertheless, I feel amazed and blessed to be the discreet and secret witness of these young couples dressed, as if in a fairy tale, to immortalize their love. It might seem a little cliché, but these theatrical scenes are very common in Taiwan and all over Asia.

Apart from the stereotypically beautiful setting, dress code, and accessories, each couple—through their style and behaviors—manages to express their inner personality through their wedding photo shoot. On certain occasions, I may encounter a timid and shy couple, and on others days, serious and formal or confident, exuberant pairs. One day I bumped into a couple that reminded me of Carmen and her torero from George Bizet's opera. They adjusted their posture under the direction of a seasoned photographer saying: "Please twist on the right, bend a little, put your right foot forward…." As if these prompts were not enough, he continued adding a long list of directions: "Put your arm a bit higher on her waist, look just above her head, smile softly…" and so on. Later, I walked twenty meters further down the lane and came across another scene quite popular among the young Taiwanese: college-aged sweethearts lovingly hold each other and a teddy bear in their arms in front of a camera.

In Taipei, as in other places in Asia, wedding photography has developed into a professional (and very profitable) institution. In my park, each couple is accompanied by a photographer, an assistant that carries sophisticated equipment in suitcases and boxes, as well as one or two make-up and prop assistants. For a few hours, the park becomes a film studio with professional teams, equipment, and costumes that express each couple's hoped-for image of romance.

Of course, the studio atmosphere might contradict with the Zen ambiance of the park. But the park belongs to every visitor, after all, and every person has his/her own vision, perception, or interest. Zen attitudes should not be a dictate nor an obligation that everyone need follow. The peaceful sensation that I cherish may only happen when sincerely respecting diversity and welcoming all that crosses my path.

Dialogue of Freedom

I belong to this group of people who speak in their head. Talking to myself is the way I process information and thoughts. It is more a dialogue with myself than a monologue.

It starts spontaneously and of course, during moments of contemplation as well. It is like hearing my own voice describe what my eyes see: the slanted branch of cherry trees, the cherry flowers, the bees nearby, the pine trees in the background, their deep, dark green color, the far off mountain with the shape of a mandarin hat, the smell of the grass crushed under my feet, the fog slowly covering the horizon. This is what a dialogue with myself sounds like in my head.

Walking by myself is, in fact, walking with myself. This "me time" allows me to experience a moment of total freedom, when I can be the person I am, totally free of any influences, out of reach from social pressures. I feel free to listen to my inner voices, free to take my time, free to let my thoughts wander, free to dream, free to close my eyes or to stare at the horizon. Just free!

I find it very soothing to let my mind alternate between modes, to let my mind freely wander between moments of contemplation, reflection, and action. Feeling, then thinking; thinking, then standing; walking slow, then fast; contemplating, then exercising, then stretching. Accepting these variations makes my experience easier, less stressful and more pleasant.

With so many seconds in one hour, if I can be fully engaged in what I feel and see for even the length of a few seconds and if this happens several times during my one hour walk, those few seconds repeated many times make for a fairly good amount of meditative time. Even if I get distracted by ongoing thoughts, I can still find a significant amount of mind space, peace, and true connection with my inner self and with the world around.

Fog & Mist

O n rainy, foggy days, the park is bathed in a mysterious atmosphere. Crystal droplets of rain hang on spider webs and make their thin canvas more visible and captivating, literally and in the figurative sense as well. My sensations shift from shiver to amazement, and the two combined together. I had never thought that I would love the spectacle of spider webs.

The entire mountain range becomes wrapped in a feathery quilt, giving wings to my imagination. I fantasize that I am an eagle flying over the valley towards the hilltop. My flight pierces the fog to finally plunge through the thick cotton clouds toward the mountain peak. The eagle's piercing eyes have the ability to see through the mist, spot the smallest details, and finally embrace the whole scenery of the clear valley hidden under the blanket of clouds.

Walking in the fog brings me a delectable new experience: the freedom of day dreaming and the unleashed imagination. Am I becoming mystical?

The Gift of Kindness

At some point during my life, while occupied by the daily struggles, I lost sight of what was truly good for me. My physical and mental needs sometimes contradicted with "real life" needs of work, familial responsibilities, personal achievement, etc. In our human world, which often feels very un-human, benevolence, peace, and freedom are given very little value. Under the rush, stress, and social pressures, listening to my very own needs—recognizing and identifying them—sometimes required more lucidity and determination than I could muster. Attending to those needs also often required painful compromise.

I have too seldom listened to my needs for sleep. Like most mothers on Earth, how could I kindly indulge myself with an early night or a lazy late morning when just a single night of full, sound sleep had long become a memory of the past? Meanwhile, I also conformed too easily to the idea that to be in shape you have to practice more sports or physical activities. I also subscribed to the common belief that if I am not good at something, it is probably due to a lack of practice. It took me years to finally give up tennis, aerobics, jogging—all of the exercises that only resulted in aching muscles, boredom, and little sense of achievement for me.

At the very beginning, when I started to walk, some unknown impetus told me to treat my body and mind with kindness. Unconsciously, I was inviting myself to be kind, to become my own best friend. It was an invitation to let sensations and emotions to come and go without trying to retain anything, an invitation to stop fighting or pushing against myself, to give myself a moment not for action nor force nor controlling situations and people. It was and still is an invitation for empathy and benevolence, for appreciation and love. Love for the light, the wind, the view—love for life, the flow of my breath, the feel of my feet on the ground…

There will be other times in the day to mobilize my energy in the fight for life, work, or greater influence…but when I walk, this moment is for me and only me.

Returning

fter an entire summer away in France, I am excited to go back and to reconnect with "my" park, the beauty of nature as well as with my own self.

When I walk out of my door, I am struck by the intensity of the sunlight. I wear my sunglasses and hat; I even carry a small umbrella, a common practice in Asia on a sunny day. With that clever equipment, the heat is not as bad as one may think. My mind still wanders between what I notice around me and what occupied me during the previous hours and recent days, but it does not take me long to be fully present and to walk in mindfulness. Now after three years into my practice, I notice with delight how natural it is to slip back into my routine. Moreover, with the regular practice it has become easier and almost instantaneous to retrieve my connection with nature. After a long absence, I also find that my eyes see anew and can capture many small differences between the environments in France and Taiwan. The light is different, as well as the temperature and the vegetation.

I walk to the end of a garden and find the shady spot that I love. I check on my familiar tree friends and the scenery. The mountain in the distance appears through some branches and even though it is a very familiar view, it captivates me. Very spontaneously, I start my breathing and stretching exercises; I am delighted to recognize the old sensations coming back to me.

I walk again, zigzagging between shady spots and sunny areas. I stop, I look, and walk again, drifting between observation and contemplation. I can spot every change in the park's organization.

This past summer, the park management has undertaken major landscaping work—clearing the undergrowth, planting new plots, changing some flowerbeds as well as renewing the pavement of certain alleys. I feel privileged to be a witness to this park's everyday life as well as to its evolution, to see new trees planted and new arrangements coming to life.

Returning gives me this lovely feeling of old sensations and new observations, a mix of habit and rediscovery—the comfort of the well-known and the surprise of the novelty.

Transition in the Air

When October comes—after months of damp summer days and nights when stepping into the outdoors feels like entering a giant steam bath—my skin imperceptibly begins a return to its normal state. The rain, at last, starts to have a refreshing quality, and sometimes a reinvigorating breeze soothes the sticky sensation on my skin. Some mornings, clouds blanket the mountains.

I don't hear the shrill sounds of the winged creatures hidden in the bushes; the cicadas are slowing down. From the change in intensity of their singing pattern, I can feel that transition is in the air. Sometimes completely silent, they seem to have taken a break. Starting this season, they have to share the park sound track with other creatures. The cicadas' hissing alternates with other invisible insects' "tic tac" song. Then, birds also begin to timidly take over. Gradually, the cicadas' chorus is replaced by newcomers from the north—flocks of birds making a stop on their way toward more tropical countries. Having no other option than to share their symphonic territory, the cicadas stay civilized and take turns singing with the others.

And one day, I hear only the birds chirping. Autumn is coming and with it, the sounds in the park are slowing down.

The park is no exception to autumn pursuing its course and every expression of natural life slowly begins to fall asleep.

The change of seasons is no surprise to anyone, and yet, during my first year walking, I am caught by the fact that it is the first autumn in which I am aware of the change of seasons through the voices of nature around me. If I were not walking daily, I would not be aware of those tiny details. I would only see the most visual cues but not hear, feel, and smell the coming of autumn. Being able to discern ordinary but delicate and beautiful phenomena fill my day with great satisfaction...and even a sense of achievement.

Thunder Showers

I love to walk in the rain and wind. The sudden gust of wind and the changing direction of whirlwinds feel invigorating. The leaves shiver more than I do. The sky glows with a white light that comes down from the clouds, and if I look through the nude branches, the dark silhouette of the wet tree against the white sky designs a dramatic figure like an old, vintage black and white photo. Under the shining drops of water, the vegetation appears different too. The shiny leaves and mirrored surfaces of water puddles sparkle everywhere, like crystal pearls or diamonds.

I don't fear getting wet. I feel the enthusiasm of being part of the natural elements, especially when, without warning, a light rain swings to violent intensity; and this sudden variation brings me an enjoyment mixed with goose bumps. I can feel the itch to jump in puddles, and I recognize the child hidden in me, as if I were a 6 year-old, fearlessly playing in the rain before going home to be scolded by adults.

Touch

Have you ever touched a camellia flower? Have you ever caressed the petals of the flower, stroked them gently and softly, and felt their smooth skin? Their texture is amazingly firm and thick, while the surface is silky and soft like powder. The contrast in sensations is quite surprising!

I can't believe it took me weeks, months, and even several seasons before I imagined that I could touch flowers. It is so much easier to stay in our comfort zone. By fearing the unknown, we fail to express our curiosity.

Camellia flowers are not at all the weak and delicate little things that many people assume. Yes, their beauty is delicate, their buds have an ephemeral life—after one day, the edges of its petals start to change color to a rusty tone. However, camellias are quite robust and strong; they are made to withstand natural forces—rain, wind, and even snow sometimes.

They are the first flowers that dare to blossom before spring comes around the corner. Before the flower blooms, the bud is closed—hard and dense—like a little stone. Then, the flower will bloom with incredible colors into a complex design of petal shapes and arrangements. Also, the camellia is uniquely robust in that the flower will keep its shape and all its petals united even when it falls. The flower will lie on the ground as a whole flower, and so, sometimes, I come across the ground covered with what looks to be a carpet of colorful flowers.

Through touching the petal, I could feel the camellia's strength and delicateness all at once. I realized that touching them does not harm them. Nature and human can find ways to connect with each other. We live in the same world.

Life Cord

Dear Camphor Tree,

Thank you for our special connection, close and intimate, from my very first day.

I remember my first impressions and my emerging emotions during the beginning phases of my walks, particularly my first time coming through the entrance of this place that I would come to think of as "my" park. You were standing right across the gate and I could not miss you—big and majestic.

Your presence was soothing and appeasing. You helped opened all my senses and awakened my attention toward every fellow tree in the park and beyond.

Over the many days I have walked under your protection, I have developed an affectionate relationship with you and with other brother and sister trees that have been the kind witnesses of my daily walks. I see you as companions. I watch you more than I look at you—actually I observe, stare, gaze, and gape at you. You may not look at me in return, but I speculate, suspect, imagine that you sense my presence. You are aware of my visit and may be acknowledging it in some invisible ways—invisible to the human eyes, at least.

You know me well, you know that I like to talk to you. You know that I touch your bark and leaves to feel their texture, but also to try to figure out what you feel—painfully wet after a thunderstorm or hydrated just right after a gentle rain. You exemplify life, you mirror human life, you make me feel alive—part of the living world.

And now I must prepare to leave you, as I am moving away from Taiwan after so many years here. It is painful to write those two words—moving, leaving—I feel ashamed or perhaps guilty to leave you and the park. You see I don't dare to write "my" park anymore. I know you will continue your life, and the camellias will continue to blossom every year before spring's arrival. I know I will eventually settle into my life in another country. But I will always continue to feel our special connection as I walk under the shades of your fellow brothers and sisters around the world. They may even tell me something about you.

I am incredibly grateful to you, dear camphor tree. From now on, I do not watch trees in the same way as before. It goes further than a way of looking at something. It is more than a different perspective. This special affection that I have nurtured for you and for every tree acts like a strong umbilical cord, tying and anchoring me with the natural world. My walk with you has gotten me closer to the essential.

Thank you.

Part II: Poems &

Invitations for Walking

How I Walk in Mindfulness

I walk and breathe,

Free pace, natural breath, intuitive walk,

Focus on breathing, observing,

Body sensations, posture, gravity,

Pressure on my feet,

Textures of the ground,

Rhythm;

Let it be, let all thoughts come and go,

Accepting, looking at them,

Focusing on present moment, current sensation,

Just walk and breathe;

Stop, inhale, look around,

What catches my eyes?

Shapes, colors, movement,

Life all around;

Let it be, let my thoughts come and go,

Watch them, let them roam,

Focus back here and now;

Walk again, stop, close my eyes,

Listen, what do I hear?

Layers of sounds, far and near,

Pleasant, unpleasant,

Identify the nature of the sounds,

Their music, rhythm, intensity, location,

Where are they from?

Let it be,

May my thoughts come and go,

Look at them and let them go,

Come back now and come back here;

Breathe, walk,

Focus on the sensations of air, in and out,

What sensation? And where?

Any smell?

Let it be,

Let my thoughts come and go

Look at them and let them go

being here and now,

nothing more and nothing less.

Standing Meditation

Observation

Attention

Birds

A flock of them

Chirping

Flying around

Several birds singing the same melody

One bird with a different song

The smell of sweet osmanthus

Ephemeral

Fragrance

Two seconds only

Then gone

The wind whirling

The light in the branches

The shade on the ground

The birds again

Off to another bush

Back to this one

The smell again

The wind again

Then the calm

The sound of an engine in the far

The sound of a truck on the road

A motorbike loud

Again, my attention to the trees

The smell

The surroundings

And the cycle goes on....

Consciousness

My mind is full of thoughts,

One thought bringing another,

Without apparent logic,

It is like a long train,

Each wagon being one thought.

Why one comes before the other?

I do not know,

No order, no apparent logic,

Until I stand and stare at them,

Then seeing them in a different light,

I distance myself,

I observe like a witness,

I can talk to myself: "Haha! You are thinking of...."

My thoughts cannot catch me, I am catching them,

I have the freedom to choose,

To choose when

It is time to think

And when it is my time to feel.

Mindful Breathing

We breathe all the time,

I may observe and contemplate my breathing anytime,

Mindful breathing does not require anything,

I may sit, lie down, stand and even walk,

When waking in the morning, at any time in the day or before sleeping,

But also, in the street, on an office chair, in a waiting room, in a car, a bus....

I put my hand on the center of my abdomen,

Sometimes I cross my arms,

embracing my rib cage,

I close my eyes but not always,

I feel the air in and out,

I observe attentively,

This alternating movement,

Similar to the wave on the shore,

Coming and going in a perpetual motion,

Fascinating, each of them being unique,

With their own length and intensity,

I might drift away, dream, and then come back,

Feeling the sensations in my body,

Trying to identify each of them,

What are they?

Where are they?

Connecting deeply with what is tangible,

What is present now,

Always bringing back my attention to my breath,

Inhale, exhale,

It might be ten breaths, or less,

It might last three minutes, or thirty,

It does not matter,

As each breath is so mindful....

Free to Choose

An invitation to be free

free to choose

to experiment with anything

free to decide for myself

when and where

free to choose my pace

free to sit on a bench

to close my eyes

keep one hand at my side

just to feel the tempo of my breath

Free to like or dislike

to be focused and not

to be conscious or unconscious

of my wandering thoughts

I have all the rights to think what I think

to be mindful or not,

to feel annoyed, excited or sad

maybe I prefer to run, jump or climb the hill,

feel out of breath and hear my heartbeats fast and furious

I am free to choose

to give one more try

to come back every day or sometimes

I am free to choose

What feels good for me and just for me.

Where Curiosity Takes Me

To question myself and to ask questions,

To read books, letters, articles, pieces of articles,

To look at photography,

To "Google," to "Wikipedia," and to search through other sources,

To visit museums,

To listen to music,

To talk, to listen, to discuss, to argue,

To think in silence,

To speak to myself, often and a lot,

To think out loud,

To chitchat,

To make friends, to keep them, to cherish them,

To love the people I love,

To love life, to love the world, the sky, the stars,

To walk, to hike, to ski,

To do yoga, Pilates,

To try,

To try just to see what will happen,

To draw, to do new activities, new jobs,

To travel to discover places, people, food,

To travel to see things I have never seen,

To travel to do things I have never done,

To search again, and search for meaning,

To understand sometimes,

To live!

Afterword: About the Artwork

I might be perceived as naïve and innocent, but I cannot help marveling at the beauty and magic of nature. I indulge myself in staring at small animals, new green leaves, or a majestic camphor tree, amazed by the complexity and perfection of different forms of life.

As I was walking in my park, I could not refrain from shooting a quick snapshot at the subjects of my admiration. Was it because I wanted to keep the memory of that moment? Not really, nor did I care too much to share it on social media! What I feel when I take a photo is more an irrepressible instinct. This beauty is so stunning that I must take a shot of it!

Taking photos is engaging in a dialogue with the elements of that scene, as if I am talking to them: "Wahoo! You are so pretty, look at your leaves. They are so perfectly cut, the complexion of your skin is incredibly bright. What a color! I can't believe my eyes…." It is a way to celebrate beauty, to pay homage to the exceptional beauty of the scene.

I have questioned myself about the coherence between taking photos and the essence of my contemplative walk. Does photography distract me from being present? Upon some reflection, I realized not at all. On the contrary I feel an intimate connection with my photo subject. Furthermore, my walk is a free space with no aims and no prohibitions either.

So, I have taken hundreds of photos. Once, at my desk, as I was writing this book, I began playing with the photos. I realized that I would have loved to draw or paint the scenes of my park, but I do not have that skill. However, I enjoyed exploring the possibilities of digital art work and I learned about a smartphone application that has helped me transform my photos into digital paintings.

All the images in this book are the product of my own work: the photographs were taken with my mobile phone and then edited through the application, Prisma. More images can be found on Instragram: *my.urban.oasis*

Table of Contents

Part II: Poems & Invitations for Walking   **83**

Made in the USA
Monee, IL
23 November 2019